ATTRACTION MARKETING (WHAT IS IT)

and What Does it Offer You?

By ALEX ANDRÉ

CONTENTS

RESIGNATION

Copyright 2019
By ALEX ANDRÉ

WHAT IS ATTRACTION MARKETING?

A s first definition, Attraction marketing is the process of drawing interest to a company, product or service using carefully devised techniques. The goal is to attract potential customers to the way the item has bettered the seller's own life.

In others words, Attraction marketing may be the buzz word that is out there commonly heard by most Internet marketers. Yet, what does this mean? As an Internet marketer, you do need to know what this type of marketing is as it will likely be one of the most important, profitable tools you have in low cost online marketing that is highly effective.

First, understand what it is and then learn how to implement it within your own business. Most business owners can find success using this method to help them to develop their online business.

It works in any sector, industry or niche. When applied effectively, it is a low cost, long term success tool no marketer should go without.

WHAT IS IT?

The short definition of what attraction marketing is may seem too simple. It is simply a term that means that the Internet marketer uses the Internet to help attract people to the business they are in.

To take this to another level, attraction marketing can be defined as bringing people to you rather than going after them. The best way to see this is to take a look at the opposite method, the way that most print or "non online" advertising is done.

In traditional advertising, countless dollars are spent to find the consumer most likely to invest in the product or service. Billboards are placed along freeways for radio stations, for example, since people listen to the radio most often in the car. Advertisements go to the most likely consumer rather than the consumer coming to the product directly for a need.

In attraction marketing, the consumer comes to you and your product or service because they have heard that it is something that can benefit them, in some way. Ultimately, this allows for the business to do well since the advertisements are being presented in a pleasant manner. Internet marketing is not often about catchy slogans and flashy ads. Rather, it is a method of bringing people into information, products and services because they are already interested. Mastering this can help a business to grow quickly.

THE QUESTION IS: DOES IT WORK?

Does attraction marketing work? The short answer to this question is yes, but there are plenty of fantastic examples of how it works. One good one is to consider the election of Mr. Obama. Regardless of whether you are from the U.S. or not, and no matter what side of the ticket you were rooting for, one thing has to be said. Mr. Obama's ability to use Internet marketing, including attraction marketing methods, helped him win this election, according to many professionals.

Obama used the various tools in Internet marketing to help him to win his election because he and his campaign moreover knew the importance and success it could bring. The world goes to the web to learn what it needs to, in today's culture. More so, the Internet provides an easy, affordable way to reach millions of people every single day. No other medium offers this.

The question is, how did Obama use attraction marketing to win the Presidential Election of the United States? Using attraction marketing tools, websites, and even things like GoogleAds helped him to make it happen.

In fact, Twitter.com was used by Mr. Obama as one of the many methods of attraction marketing he used. By gaining a huge following and communicating through them in short clips, he could converse with everyday people, put his message out and do it all without spending a penny for it.

The concept of attraction marketing is very simple. Put the relationship first. Provide something of value. Develop trust, build a great rapport before you attempt to sell anything to anyone. Network marketing is a relationship-based business. So, your priority when making new contacts is to focus on developing relationships.

We believe the last thing you want to do is to pitch them on your opportunity before they even get to know you. One of the quickest and easiest ways to build rapport and get people to like you is to give people something of value. This can be a referral, contact, or benefit that will help them.

So, who do you want to attract? Who is your target market? Our target market is the group of people we want to attract to our business.

Ask yourself, who is your ideal customer? Who would be best suited to join your business? Or better yet, who would be best suited to succeed in your business? Once you have your target market figured out, you need to find a way to attract them to you. We do that by adding value to their lives.

Figure out what their problems are by first listening to them. Your target market will tell you what's bugging them if you listen to their conversations. Find out where they are gathering (in person or online) and join the conversation. Once you have found out what several problems are, pick one that you are passionate about and research to find the answer for it.

Try adding value to their lives by solving their problems. Give them the answers to the issues that are bothering them. Once you have the best answer to that problem, offer the solution to your target market. Your solution has value to your potential customers. Providing value makes you stand out and positions you as a leader.

Rinse and repeat the above steps. Continue to create value by providing solutions to their problems. Over time, this will build up a relationship with your potential customers and eventually you will be in the position to offer them a product or service they can buy from you, or maybe even join you and your business opportunity

Another example of this is Facebook. Everyone on the web knows that Facebook.com is a heaven for younger generation individuals who like to find each other and chat. The trend has grown. In fact, businesses, politicians, and even employers are using it as a tool to connect with others. Mr. Obama's Facebook page was yet another form of attraction marketing that helped him to get his message out.

As you can see, there are excellent ways that attraction marketing works. For most of the general public, you aren't trying to win the presidential election. Nevertheless, this tool can still be used to help virtually anyone to gain success in getting traffic to their website.

APPLYING ATTRACTION MARKETING METHODS
TO YOUR BUSINESS

Any Internet marketer can apply the lessons learned to their own Internet business. There are three main parts to developing a successful attraction marketing campaign, but the good news is that none of them are difficult, costly or overly time consuming.

Here, we'll explore these three parts and find out how you can put them to use no matter what type of Internet marketing business you have.

In short, they are as follows:

> - Consumers find you, your products or services on the web.
> - Consumers allow you to contact them.
> - You provide consumers with information they can use and benefit from, through email, and keep

your business in front of them all the time.
To better understand how to do this, keep reading.

PART 1: CONSUMERS FIND YOU

The first step in the process is to get people to find you online. Remember, with attraction marketing, they are coming to you. You are not going out searching for them and advertising directly. So, how do you get more people to find you online?

WEBSITE DESIGN FIRST

There are several ways to accomplish this. First, the ultimate first step is to have a useful website and/or blog where you can talk with, work with and interact with your visitors. You will need to ensure it is information based rather than a sales gimmick. Online, sales gimmicks, long sized sales letters are less likely to work than other methods of marketing, especially in attraction marketing. Make sure your website tells visitors that you are providing a service to them, information to them and not a sales ad to convince them to buy.

ARTICLE DIRECTORIES

Next, you will need to get your information out there. For example, develop excellent articles and detailed outlines related to your business or product and then get it out into the mainstream.

You can post them on various article directories.

The benefit of doing this is two-fold. Due to the extreme popularity of many of these websites, Google ranks articles quickly there and many get first page Google results if they are optimized properly. This means that when someone looking for information on a product or service you are offering searches for it in Google, chances are good your article will pop up as a result.

Another benefit is that quality article directories work for what their intended purpose is. That purpose is to allow webmasters to pick up these articles (with your resource box on them) and use them on their websites or in their blogs. Their readers instantly get to read what you are talking about and they can click on the link and take it back to your website where they can buy what you are offering.

Yet another extension of this is the ability to get that golden back link to your website. This alone helps to boost your website's ranking in Google's search engines, and in other search engines. The more back links pointing into your website, the more people will find you and the better Google ranks your website. And, all you have done is write an article.

SOCIAL NETWORKING WEBSITES

From this point, there are many other ways to build that successful attraction marketing. One of the most attractive, enjoyable ways to get your business out there is, in fact, to talk about it! Social networking is what it sounds like. It is a method of communicating with others about anything you want to, really.

Most social networking websites where not started to help businesses to grow, but most of them are able to be used this way. Going back to our example, Mr. Obama used many of them to get to his people.

This is what you are looking for, too. You are looking for a way to give people information. Once they have that information, they can then come to you to get what they need. This works in any type of Internet niche, too.

Human nature by default has been programmed to be socially active to a certain extent. Some people are more active, while others are less so!
However, people have always been looking for ways to connect and network with each other. And, in this age of digitisation, people have found ways to be socially active on the internet, which is possible with the advent of the numerous social networking platforms and apps.

Now, even relationships begin, grow and end on social media. People no longer need a personal handshake or face-to-face meeting.

Social media sites have also grown in numbers by leaps and bounds. As per the statistics revealed on Statista, approximately 2 billion users used social networking sites and apps in 2015. And, with the increased use of mobile devices, this number is likely to cross the 2.9 billion mark by 2019.

Social networking sites include any of the following:

- ___Digg.com___
Find useful articles and blog postings and Digg them. The more Digg's received, the more people will read the article and therefore come to the website.

- **_Whatsapp_**

Network with others while also getting more traffic to your website as people "Stumble upon it" through the company's tools.

- **_Facebook.com_**

Great for meeting, socializing and talking about yourself, your business or anything else. Connect with thousands of people here.

- **_MySpace.com_**

Share all sorts of information, connect with others, networking with others with comparative businesses and by all means, subtly link to your website.

- **_YouTube.com_**

Great for informational videos and socializing. Who doesn't want to watch a few YouTube videos every now and then? Use them to help market your business indirectly.

- ***Twitter.com***

Type in short messages (only sometimes containing a link) to let others know what you are doing throughout the day. Network and build up the number of Tweets you are following. Addictive, but highly beneficial once you've built a successful following on Twitter.

- ***Skype***

Skype, owned by Microsoft, is one of the most popular communication-based social networking platforms. It allows you to connect with people through voice calls, video calls (using a webcam) and text messaging. You can even conduct group conference calls. And, the best part is that Skype-to-Skype calls are free and can be used to communicate with anyone, located in any part of the world, over the internet.

- ***Viber***

This multi-lingual social platform, which is available in more than 30 languages, is known for its instant text messaging and voice messaging capabilities. You can also share photos and videos and audio messages, using Viber. It offers you the ability to call non-Viber users through a feature named Viber Out.

- *Pinterest*

This is a photo sharing and visual bookmarking social media site or app that enables you to find new ideas for your projects and save them. So, you can do DIY tasks or home improvement projects, plan your travel agenda and so on by using Pinterest..

- *LinkedIn*

LinkedIn is easily one of the most popular professional social networking sites or apps and is available in over 20 languages. It is used across the globe by all types of professionals and serves as an ideal platform to connect with different businesses, locate and hire ideal candidates, and more. It boasts over 400 million members.

- *Instagram*

Instagram was launched as a unique social networking platform that was completely based on sharing photos and videos. This photo sharing social networking app thus enables you to capture the best moments of your life, with your phone's camera or any other camera, and convert them into works of art.

This is possible because Instagram allows you to apply multiple filters to your photos and you can easily post them to other popular social networking sites, such as Facebook and Twitter. It is now part of the Facebook empire

There are many, many more websites that can be used like this. The key is to really use those where you think the best results can be found, but also where you find yourself enjoying it.

To find more of these social networking websites, visit this Wikipedia pages: http://en.wikipedia.org/wiki/List_of_social_networking_websites or https://makeawebsitehub.com/social-media-sites/

There is no way that you can go to all of these websites, but the key is not to invest all of your time in them, either. You should find one, two, or three to really dive into and to work with.

THE NECESSITY OF BUILDING A NETWORK

It Allows You to Help Others. One of the most important benefits of networking that people tend to overlook is that it allows you to help other people. Granted, our motives in the professional world are rarely altruistic, but helping someone else with their career goals can be truly rewarding.

While it is essential for individuals to build a network of people to get traffic to their website, it is often something that is failed out. For example, let's say you join Facebook.com, put up a few pictures, find your email contacts and then don't do much else. No one is going to find you that can help you to build your business.

You need to network and build a sizable following or allow others to find you on any of these websites by providing concise yet useful information. For example, you create a login at Digg.com, a social networking website that works quite indirectly for getting visitors to websites. You start to submit articles to Digg.com allowing for others to find them through the company's normal means. You wait. You don't see too much traffic there. Oh, well... you move on.

This is where the mistake happens. The fact is, you have to get out there and really make your presence known. Here are some tips to make this possible.

- Use your profile!
  This is one of the key tools you have to get people back to your website. Be sure to use keywords you would associate with your business in your profile, but make it informal. There is no room for sales here.

- Socialize with others
  Find others at the website that share something in common with you and build a network with them. For example, you may be promoting a baby product and you are a mother. When you join the website, promote yourself as a mother first, connecting with other mothers at the website.

- Build a network from your friend's networks
  Let's say you use your email contacts and locate them on your favourite social sites. That's great. Don't stop there. Befriend not just these individuals but also their friends, too. Keep going, building a network for yourself the whole time.

There are many ways to build a network using social medium. The key is to keep working at it and enjoying the process. Over time, people come to your website to find out what you have to offer. This gets them interested and they buy from you. The process works like this many times over and at the end of the day, you have drawn people to you without talking too much about your business.

PART 2: GETTING PERMISSION TO COMMUNICATE

Permission means to give formal consent to another person. When using email to market your business, you want to have permission from your prospects and customers.

T he next step in the process of using attraction marketing to your advantage is to get people to let you talk to them. With the advent of laws regarding spam and other inappropriate means of communication, it has become very important for any Internet marketer to be sure they stay on the good side of the law.

As an Internet marketer, you need to have the permission of a consumer, client or website visitors to send them any form of communication other than direct communication such as through a blog comment.

Why you should do this, you may be asking. As part of the process of developing a successful Internet marketing business, you need to get your product or service in front of the client. As you will see in Part 3, this is the key to your success in selling.

There are many ways that this can be done. The bottom line is that it has to be done. You want those that find you on the web to come to your website and a lead capture page, for example. This way, you are able to get their permission to send them more information.

There are many lead capture tools available to help you to accomplish this including The Renegade and Marketing Merge, for example. You can also create your own, and not something that is difficult to do on your own, even if you are not a techie.

What happens is simple:
- Individuals find your information on the web.
- They follow it to your website's lead capture page.
- They sign up when they arrive there.

You have a lead to sell to, market to or otherwise use.

Now, you can advertise to them.

PART 3: PROVIDE INFORMATIONAL EMAILS TO THE CUSTOMER

N ow that you have gone through all of this work, you still do not have a profit in hand. Why not?

This is where the final part of the three part process of using attraction marketing comes in. Now, you will take the information and resources that you have worked so hard to develop and make them into something that's going to turn a profit for you.

Keep in mind that while this process may seem like it is long and has a lot of work to it, you are going to automate much of it and secondly, you are going to do all three things at one time. This way, you are likely to start making money from attraction marketing right from the beginning of starting the process.

INFORMATIONAL, NOT SPAM

One of the keys to building a successful attraction marketing plan is not to be overly sales like. Everything and anything that you do should be done based on subtle sales information. You are providing information to the client. You are not hard selling what you have to offer to them. This is why it is called attraction marketing. The consumer is attracted to you because you are giving them valuable information and tools to use.

Don't fail on that point: informational is key, not sales ads.

DEVELOP A PLAN

As part of the process of using the permissions given to you by those who have visited your website, you will need a plan. The plan is quite specific. You need to send emails to those who are on your list that allow them to gain something and learn something. You need to have a plan in place so that you can be professional while still getting people to your website at the same time.

In this form of attraction marketing, you are attracting people to your website by first telling them something important. They think, "Hey, this is great. This is just what I need." They then head over to your website from the link posted in the email. They can then make a purchase from you or do what you wish for them to do.

To make sure this happens, you need to ensure that your emails are well received and that they have the best information they can offer to the reader. This way, they are most likely to visit your website.

CONSTRUCTING EMAILS

The first step in the process is to develop a newsletter or other email communication with them. It does not matter what you call it. Rather, it matters what is in it. Here are some examples of quality content to provide to your readers.

- Provide Informational Articles
Your clients want to read something helpful to them. They want to read something that teaches them something. For example, let's say you are selling an informational product on acne. In your email message to your readers, you write about the causes of acne. This provides them with some type of information.

- Make your subject line effective
A common problem that many people have when using any form of email marketing is that they just do not get

their readers to open up the email. How can you do well if the reader is not even reading what you have to offer? Use your subject line as a tool. In the above example, the subject line could be, "what causes acne and what you can do about it now."

- Make your email personal
If you have ever opened up an email and read it knowing that they were just selling something, chances are good the information with was a simple made up, canned response. That's boring and actually worthless. Use the reader's names. Be sure to write to them, not to academics. Be personal, yet professional at the same time.

- Don't overdo it with graphics
Another problem with email marketing like this is that people go overboard with graphics. You have seconds to impress your reader and get them to actually read the email you have sent. If you have so many graphics within it that it takes forever to load, they will close the email and move on long before actually seeing what you were going to talk about.

- Tell them what to do
Perhaps the most important aspect of any email used like this is that it has to provide your readers with a way of reacting to what you have sent. Tell them what to do or what they can do to learn more. Give them the link to follow that takes them to the answers to their questions. For example, in the above example, after detailing all of the causes of acne, follow up with a link that takes the individual to your acne cure website. The link may read, "Finally, there is help for any of these acne causes."

Attraction marketing is only as successful as you make it. Therefore, if you invest a little time in it, especially in writing these emails, chances are good you will get very little from it. Take your time to produce a quality, highly effective email that is sent to your readers.

WHAT TO SEND IN EMAILS

Still unsure of what you can do with your emails? Here are a few more ideas to work with:

- Share information on the topic you have a passion about, hopefully related to your website.
- Share a good book, informational product or other item that in some way relates to your business indirectly.
- Share live event information. Perhaps you are doing an educational seminar or a web cast and want to invite your readers to come to your website to attend.
- Perhaps you are running a sale and you wish to provide your readers with information regarding it.
- Perhaps you are providing some recorded trainings and want to share the details with your list.

That's all it takes to get the email going. An effective campaign does get people back to your website. In fact, attraction marketing can work in many ways to gain you resources including higher sales potential. Take the time to put attraction marketing in place and you will see traffic to your website come in from a variety of sources. You are likely to see your sales go up as long as you have provided your readers with the helpful tools and resources they need to make wise decisions.

If you are not sure if it can work for you, consider traditional sales mechanisms. You could pay a heavily trafficked website for an ad in the thousands of dollars range and hope to get enough readers back to your website. Or, you can invest your time, not your money, in getting quality traffic that is already interested in you!

www.ingramcontent.com/pod-product-compliance
Lightning Source LLC
Chambersburg PA
CBHW031250050326
40690CB00007B/1037